After Villon

Also by Roger Farr

Surplus (2006)
Means (2012)
IKMQ (2012)
I Am a City Still But Soon I Shan't Be (2019)

AFTER VILLON

Roger Farr

NEW STAR BOOKS | VANCOUVER | 2022

NEW STAR BOOKS LTD
No. 107–3477 Commercial St, Vancouver, BC V5N 4E8 CANADA
1574 Gulf Road, No. 1517 Point Roberts, WA 98281 USA
newstarbooks.com · info@newstarbooks.com

Copyright Roger Farr 2022. All rights reserved. No part of this work may be reproduced, stored in a retrieval system or transmitted, in any form or by any means, without the prior written consent of the publisher or a licence from Access Copyright.

The publisher acknowledges the financial support of the Canada Council for the Arts, the British Columbia Arts Council, and the Government of Canada.

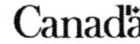 Canada Council   Conseil des arts
for the Arts   du Canada

Supported by the Province of British Columbia

Cataloguing information for this book is available from Library and Archives Canada, www.collectionscanada.gc.ca.
ISBN: 978-1-55420-187-7

Cover design by Oliver McPartlin
Typeset by New Star Books
Royal 1 D X f. 2v Dream of the Magi (p. 59) © British Library Board
Printed and bound in Canada by Imprimerie Gauvin, Gatineau, QC

First printing April 2022

For Dianna

&
Huguette du Hamel

First Letter   4
Everything But Myself   6
Ballad of Erotic Misery   8
Ballad for Friends, With Benefits   10
Ballad of Non-cooperation   12
11   14
27   15
36   16
Ballad of the Pea and the Shell   17
La Belle Hëaulmiere   18
Compario   21
All Standard Language Shall Be Fried   24
Ballad of Counter-truths   26
Second Letter   28
Five Ballads in Jargon   31
    Translator's Note   32
        I   34
        II   36
        III   38
        IV   40
        V   42

Rondel 44
Ballad in A Minor 45
24 47
Ballad of Negations 48
Third Letter 50
18 52
Danse Macabre 53
Ballad of the Fourth Mode 55
39 57
63 58
Fourth Letter 60
Passages from "Le Lais" 62
90 64
16 65
Fifth Letter 66
Rondel 67
159 68

Acknowledgements 69

Objects, words must be led across time not preserved against it.
— Jack Spicer

There is a form. Not to break it every once in a while is stupid. Not to honor it on the other hand is to ask for trouble. If these two notions can be kept in the head at all times it can never go completely bust.

— Jean Callais

Selon le clerc est deu le maistre.

— François Villon

Ioncheurs ionchans en ioncherie
Rebignez bien ou ioncherez
Quostac nembroue vostre arerie
Ou accolles sont voz ainsnez
Poussez de la quille et brouez
Car tost seriez rouppieux
Eschec quacollez ne soies
Par la poe du marieux.

Cheaters cheating cheats
take a good look at your teachers
or you-know-who will mount
your derrière & put a ring on your
neck. Seriously you'll be sorry
if you don't "widen your stride"
& save your hide before
the Hangman ends your poem.

Villon,

Language is a game in which the rules are known only to the players.

When I translate one of your poems & come across a word I don't understand, I bluff. Sometimes I win, sometimes you lose. I recognize only a few words of the language you wrote in. Some of them were counterfeits coined by you & never seen again. We both cheat.

It's all very difficult. I want to decipher the form of life, the game, not the "objects." I also seek some advice about *vice*. The problem is some of the codes may have been cracked by cops, & we both know better than to trust a poem in which the poet *sings*.

I'm getting weary of cheaters cheating cheats. Mash something up. Swap the dice. Pretend it's new. Poets aren't murderers. We're *executioners*. Honour among thieves. This is what is meant by "the Tradition."

Most of my contemporaries hate poetry. They get up early, write their poems in the dark, bear down on the meaning of every word, churn the words around in their mouths, gargle with different words, then spit it out in an email addressed to someone doing the exact same thing across town. Others find poems among the Wires. They have no control over their digits, don't know how to stop. That's the worst.

Villon, you're not a straight talker – your words are queer. You use words to communicate ideas to certain people, while deceiving others. It's as though you're playing a Game: your poems are not the game, but rather the means for one. Your words are codes, or cards. I suspect the manner in which you deal them holds the secret.

That is what I must translate: an *arrangement*. It requires new methods. The odds aren't good. But I might get lucky.

I repeat – we both cheat.

— RF

Everything But Myself

I know a racket from a numbers game
I know where to find a bacon stretcher in a foyer
I know a chin check from a knock up
I know my side-dough from my overhead
I know when a swallower gets the soggy pizza
I know where the deck lizards take a powder
I know how to twist the Borden
I know everything but myself

I know a Hellmart from a Slaughterhouse
I know where to go basket shopping for a bull
I know when there's a bear at my backdoor
I know a shiny bum when I have one
I know when to wear the wig
I know if a skelm is stalking my stekkie
I know how much chalkface pays by the hour
I know everything but myself

I know the Queen of Spades from the Queen of Hearts
I know when Mr Kessler wants a Kriegspiel
I know a biblio-pimp with a blocking move
I know how the Master likes her *canelés*
I know that local yokel with the dirty docs
I know my mashes from my mash ups
I know where the gas works are
I know everything but myself

I know a button buster when I hear one
I know what buzzard bait smells like in May
I know why a lip tease leads to hard labour
I know my Patsy Cline from my Molly O'Malia
I know how to tell a smellfungus from a railbird
I know when to Warhol a sucker shuffle
I know not to bunt in the middle of a bake sale
I know everything but myself

Your honour, I know it all
I know how to dead-lurk a crib & I know the score
I know when to fold, & put an end to it all.

"The authenticity of poetry, from this point on, will be a quality residing in the variable and organic concordance between the apprehended fact and its expressed transposition. Poetry will be true if the sentiment that animates it has been intimately lived, not if it results from some received formula. It will be necessary, in short, for the poet to have lived it intensely enough for his poetic expression to be naturally adequate to it." – Tzara, "The Modernity of Villon."

Ballad of Erotic Misery

For every brittle cock there's a beard pie
For every tunnel hole a bone keeper
For every queer deal a quick querent
For every sloppy Jack a kimbo cut
For every fur fastener a posh cheeser
For every city-top a hobble jock
For every moonlighter a mooseface
For every pleasure desires eternity

For every Coco Loco there's a bolo'bolo
For every bum itch an angel arse
For every dump-a-Trump a please-a-pig
For every bazoo blower an organ bag
For every sky pilot scourge a sixty rod
For every sweathog a shush bickie
For every beaver fiddler a bit of spink
For every pleasure desires eternity

For every stool pigeon there's a goose
For every narc fink rat a cow cross cheek
For every Czolgoszizzle a Kronstadt
For every niddle-noodle a sparrow cop
For every geo Commie-funk a nose squeeze
For every crusty bogshop a BFE
For every finger gank a yum yum
For every pleasure desires eternity

For every tenter-tummy there's a bronut
For every cruggy saucebox a chuck-wow
For every lit schlemiel a Tale of Two Fograms
For every clapping fuck-fist a snudge-snout
For every electro-pony a quail-pipe
For every dolly spot a fullam toss
For every dissy-do a docent-shop
For every pleasure desires eternity

The soundtrack to this ballad consisted of rumbling coal carts, screaming fishmongers and chestnut vendors, church bells, horses and donkeys and pigs and dogs. It would be considered Romantic to suggest it was first presented in a tavern, in front of an ex- lover's house, in court, or perhaps a bath house.

Ballad for Friends, With Benefits

Say you're an allo-sucker & some
Ollopod fuck-Jack earwigs on you
at the chuckaluck: not the usual
Monogenist in a creaky bone house
you won't die by the pig's nightcap
so you count up your bindles & punch
the breeze to Regret City where you blow
them like a Silicon Cowboy at The Mule.

Or maybe you grind out homolectic
canard-cum-tracts on The New Pursies
spook the bae-gutted vampos & gas
at the doromaniacs playing it so arsy-
varsy? Suppose you're a geach & you
paunch patricians, those scuggy amen
snorters: got an alibi? Got a bobber
to dodge the trib? Watch out for tossy

prates who jaw trap in the swamps, kiss
the cosh & snickle, woke-dial Mom
& bloom or bleed the lollpoop at the fool's
wedding, shuck the red oyster while
wearing a tight cravat, remove thy floppy
scum bag mid-solo & tope. Or perhaps
you are a cheap-jack mountebank
with a bad case of zymotic satyrisis?

Friends with benefits I implore you
Always watch your frogskins
Remember the exits in the tabernacle &
Run! – unelss your bae wants a two-on-one.

In *The Secret of Villon* Tzara claimed to have discovered a "procedure" operating in Villon's poetry, in which proper names are cryptographically embedded in certain lines by use of a complex anagrammatic formula. There is some debate as to whether this "key" was a public secret in late-15th century Paris. The translator refers his Enemies to this work.

Ballad of Non-cooperation

Tell me where, or in what nephogram
Is Foo Foo, that lovely Uxorium
Apeling or Twag
Who was zir nearest chaw bag
Ericking, at the clap of a geek
Over the ringhal, & the grand tableaux
Whose bunk log toppled the holy dollar?
So…where is last year's blow?

Where is that gorky Equlibrist,
Who got goffed, to my great sho-sho
By that Picture Gallery, in the stiff bus
For love of Sir Penis with the palsy jaw
& where now is that simian Brian
Na who backed a two-wheel barrel blow
Put us in the top shelf sack & rocked?
So…where is last year's blow?

Hey where the Klan moms at?
The white sticky-bags stuffed w/ twaddle
Suckling claptrap fashy journalist
Malevolent changeling freaking in Cumbie
Or the Root Sisters with the inky think holes
The vanilla thug cream? Oh
Where is Mrs Stilwell, she who reigns?
So…where is last year's blow?

Officer, please don't ask again
Where they are – I really don't know
& have only this to say:
Where oh where is last year's blow?

The winter of 1460 in Paris was unseasonably warm and dry.
Also: "The analysis of winter precipitation before instrumental
measurement records is challenging…in many cases the
chroniclers do not clearly distinguish between the duration of
snowfall and the timespan during which the snow cover did not
melt, resulting in misinterpretations."
See also "Crack Rocks", below.

11

Also, to CUETS Mastercard
i.e. To Whom it May Concern

"it" being about $14,000
& to Ms. Dumbkin, CRA collector

I leave my spring action blade
presently for sale on Ebay
to pay a bar tab of about $70.

I want it on the books
that they both shall get the shaft.

With the exception of Perec and Tzara, poets are notoriously bad with figures.

27

Also, my Regularized PT 6
at the University

which I leave, by Resignation
to secure against hardship

to the clerks in Ottawa
mentioned above. Naturally

my charity was incited after
viewing them in the nude.

Villon received his Master of Arts degree in 1452. In terms of
our current concerns, this is significant only insofar as doing so
secured him the protection of the church, so he was no longer
subject to the penalties of civic law.

36

Sometimes when I grumble
about being broke my heart

says: "Stop the grousing, guy
you can always go on the dole

tomorrow! So you're not exactly
the Jack of Hearts – much better

to play the cards you're dealt
than leave the table on a bluff."

Certain decks of cards are composed entirely of Hearts.

Ballad of the Pea and the Shell
Le Testament (67-69)

Once deceived, I came to see how *one*
object may be exchanged for *another* –

a *gong goozler* for a *digit*
an *email* for a *bum itch*

a *Kriegspiel* for a *sailor*
a *foot long* for a *banana stick*

– & how cheats use slights & devices
to swap *verse* for *vice* & *vice versa* –

a *shanker* for a *charnel house*
a *deck of cards* for a *dolly spot*

a *tavern* for a *Tappecoue*
a *sticky bag* for a *skeleton*

– which is how *Love* deceives & leaves
us banging on the *Prison House* door.

After he delivered a fatal knife wound to the priest Sermoise on 5 June, 1455, Villon reported the incident to a local barber – using the alias "Michel Mouton" – then fled Paris. Later, in *Le Petite Testament*, he would describe this so-called *Mouton* ("mutton") as *malostru changon*, which can be translated as *unfortunate trickster* or *malevolent changeling* or perhaps *evil imposter*.

La Belle Hëaulmiere
From *Le Testament*

49

So many men have I refused
– which in retrospect was not sage –

save for loving this one tricky boy
who had all of me in a grande cup.

Sure, there were others I finessed
but by my Mother I loved him best.

He was ornamental but rude &
when he took me he was mean.

50

He would slap to bitch-train me
trample me & I'd beg for more

ride me from behind with reigns
command me to kiss him & I did

until I'd disremember being mauled.
I was a glutton for this rotten fruit

I asked for it & I'm embarrassed now
I'm left with only bruises & scars.

51

Whatever, he died thirty years ago
& I remain old & hoary & when I

look back on the good times we had
regard my old self through the new

measure an aged body in the nude
& see how much I've changed

poor dry sack of meager means
it stiffens me with rage!

52

Where is the smooth forehead
the blonde hair & sharp eyebrows

vivid eyes & jolly look that turned
every head, even the squares'?

Where's that classy nose, not too big
not too small, the accurate ears

dimpled chin, bright visage
& that million dollar mouth?

53

Those angled narrow shoulders
long arms with expert hands

torso cut like a figure from Lukacs
well-proportioned & fashioned

to hold up during our play
with an ass borrowed from de Sade

& between my thighs something
stirring in its little garden bed?

54

The brow is creased, the hair is gray
eyebrows feral & the bright eyes

that caught so many sailors, dim.
Beauty of nose is now a long thing

pendent ears with wiry hairs
pale visage tainted with mortality &

the chin – what chin? – sunken
those lovely lips just withered skin.

55

That's what beauty comes to
for each of us poor old suckers

lowering our asses to the ground
sad sacks of potatoes crowded

round a fire, passing a joint that
once aflame abruptly burns out.

We were once on fire too, but
everything ends, lovers & friends.

Compario

Villon:

> "Le front ridé, les cheveulx gris,
> Les sourcilz cheuz, les yeulx estains,
> Qui faisoient regars et ris,
> Dont maintz marchans furent attains"

Sargent-Baur:

> "The forehead wrinkled, hair turned gray,
> The eyebrows fallen, eyes grown dim,
> Which used to give out looks & smiles
> By which a lot of fools were caught."

Roderfer/Callais:

> "Now my forehead is lined like a roadmap,
> My hair is gray, my lashes fall out,
> & my eyes are glossy, the same ones which used
> To phase everyone out with their laughing glances."

Georgi:

> "That brow is wrinkled, the blonde hair grey;
> The eyebrows sag, those eyes gone dull
> Which used to laugh & flash such looks
> As shipwrecked many hapless man."

Google:

> "The wrinkled forehead, the gray
> cheveuls,
> Eyebrows cheuz,
> yeulx estains,
> Who were staring &
> laughing,
> Many merchants were
> in possession of"

Lepper:

> "The forehead wrinkled, ringlets gray,
> The eyebrows hairless, dim the eyes
> That smiled so saucily & gay
> Entrancing men of merchandise"

Lewis:

> "A riddled forehead, hair gone grey,
>   Falling eyebrows, eyes gone red & blind,
> There laughs & looks all fled away,
>   Yea, all that smote men's hearts are fled."

Kinnel:

> "The forehead lined, the hair gray
> The eyebrows all fallen out, the eyes clouded
> Which threw those bright glances
> That filled many a poor devil"

Dictation:

> "The phone region, the Chevy grease,
> The stories sure, Liz you stain,
> Key face wash regarding baby,
> Don't mate Marshawn's friend okay"

Farr:

> "The brow is creased, the hair is gray
> eyebrows feral & the bright eyes
>
> that caught so many sailors, dim."

Villon's lawyer, Jehan Cotart, spent time in the same prison as his client.

All Standard Language Shall Be Fried

In the thionazin applied to Wordsworth's daffodils
In ointment of oxydisulfoton, to a pig
Or in vapors of phenylmercuric acetate
In that opaque compound used to make diamonds
In monocrotophos mixed with an assassin's drool
In the phosphine solution which the Emperor prefers
In wave after wave of nitrogen dioxide
Shall all standard language be fried!

In vinyl acetate a.k.a the Communist Hypothesis
In balm of selenious acid
Or in pillows misted with puffs of diborane
In droplets of zinc phosphide, to draw out the rats
In hydrogen sulphide skimmed off the Athabasca River
In two parts sulfur dichloride, one part ethylene
In magnificent cathedrals of sulfur tetrafluoride
Shall all standard language be fried!

In chlorodimethyl ether derived from Epicurus' tears
In sonnets waxing upon the pale clouds of formothion
Or in crocks of Oklahoma-quality paraquat
In the demeton used to decompose the class
In mirex & dinoseb, in endrin & propoxur
In the anthracyclines of optimism
In the yolk of an egg poached in arsenic pentafluoride
Shall all standard language be fried!

The first glossary claiming to have captured the meanings of the secret jargon of the Coquillards appeared in 1455. By 1611, the first French-English dictionary would define "villon" as "cousener, conycatcher, cunning or witty rogue; a nimble nave; a pleasant theefe (for such a one was François Villon)." For some time after, "villon" signified a "cheat." Later, via a process of homophonic variation, which is a primary element of all slangs and *argots*, Villon would be "known as" a villain.

Ballad of Counter-truths

There's no shame like morality
no clarity like drunkenness
no brutishness like a saint's
no warning like a whisper
no conviction like cynicism
no pleasure like the whip
no nostalgia like utopia
no man as wise as one in love

There's no solitude like the herd's
no friend like a hustler
no dream like a blueprint
no regret like a photograph
no debt like hope
no health like a hangover
no theft like charity
no man as wise as one in love

No fate like infancy
no filth that stinks worse than purity
no sweetness like poison
no game like love
no beginning like an exit strategy
no madness like a methodology
no liar like a poet
no man as wise as one in love

Friends, what is it that you desire?
Affirmations & assurances?
Rest & relaxation is what I see in your cards
Rejoice!

In which the poet demonstrates his Superior Intelligence by mocking universal knowledge and the spooks of Truth, Law, and Fidelity by means of proverb, contradiction, and inversion.

Villon,

I have been speaking patiently to our contemporaries, some of whom remain home-town Heroes. Others speak merely to be listened to, & they write about anything: love & grief & trauma & art. My letters to them have not been coming lately – I need sleep – & I am losing interest in their Pantheon, which appears always in the forms of quotations in prose. They publish this prose.

This is not prose.

Saying this brings a calmness over me, enough that I may now digest the last letter you slipped inside Book Six of *De Proprietatibus Rerum*. Thank you for that. I will fence it for more than a few *sous*.

I read nothing else in the Palace last night, except those lines you had written. Just before last call, I persuaded two drunken companions to translate them for me, for historical accuracy, & have slipped them in here:

Crack Rocks
Let a huge shot of Spunk blow off their heads;
Let the mall security clean out their Dead;
Let their bodies be torn & skinned their Asses,
Then cut their Wire with their own ashes;
& let it rain all night while they seek Shelter
Until the Heat rises to make them swelter.

> Rip off their fanny-packs & grab their Gear,
> Then let them complain in the open air;
> Stick them with needles & shank their back-sides
> Take their pre-paid Visas to the Upper East Side;
> Cross their cheeks with a Blade & do not Exonerate
> The Scum who shovel Snow with Murder 8.

Of course, my new associates have agreed to enroll in my Advanced Poetics class on translation in the Spring. I am presently making an Appeal to the King to release me from teaching it.

Villon, we require new readers – in-the-know, affiliated readers. Most readers are schooled by Tradition, & we are Tradition's enemies, be it in poetry, or anything else. We will transform what poetry is with our patience. Your letters took centuries to arrive.

I agree, we have the means to transform Tradition into what it is to be, because we would rather become poetry's aims, not the means of its disclosure. That is the job of rhetoric, & rats. Our poetry will establish, through these weak, dissatisfying letters, a new temperament, a new *Testament*.

In the last paragraph of your final letter, you wrote of a dream in which you returned home (I believe it was early in 1456), to find that everyone was speaking an obscure variant of the Common Language. By night, the poets, a sour-stomached & mean patchwork of fools, would write about Love. This Paris, this town, in this country of your unconscious, was an image of the future.

Villon, let's be naked. Our Word shall be our Bond. Not for the Courts, of course, as you learned in Angers, but among *spelicans*.

>Your Humble Clerk,
>— RF

Five Ballads in Jargon
François Villon

From Alice Becker-Ho's translations into modern French
La Part Maudite dans l'Oevure de François Villon
by Roger Farr

Translator's Note

Composed in 1455 in the wake of the Dijon Trials of fifteen Coquillards – alleged members of a criminal gang with which Villon is said to have been associated – the *Ballads in Jargon* were probably hummed for a century & a half before they were transcribed by ear. There is no guarantee of their fidelity to the original words of an author. They are sometimes attributed to Villon.

To complicate matters, the *Ballads* were composed in a secret jargon, & possibly other codes, known only to the gang. This language was said to have been popped by police during interrogations, after an informant claimed that "knowledge was entrusted to him once he began to sham allegiance to their ways." But this is a dubious claim. The subjects of interrogation were noted experts in using language to hide – *in plain sight* – ideas & instructions which could (for tactical reasons, such as interrogations), only be communicated to insiders & associates. Such a task required a mobile vocabulary able to change or camouflage itself whenever it became *visible*. From the perspective of that language, any practice of translation & interpretation is now "suspect", & so it is wise a to keep one's wits about one when approaching these poems. As Tzara notes,

> Despite the many more or less fantastical attempts that have been made at decipherment, one can only agree with Sainéan, the greatest specialist in jargon, that "all things considered, most of the terms of argot or *jobelin*

will probably remain a closed book for us, & that, forever."

There can be no question that the *Ballads* present serious lexical obstacles; however, what is recognizable at all times is their mode of address: they are illocutionary acts of *warning*, encoded messages sent to friends & accomplices telling them to stay out of the hands of the authorities, lest they be captured, incarcerated, fucked-over, whipped, & ear-notched.

With all this in mind, it can be argued that the best source for an English rendering of the *Ballads* is the recent translation from Middle into Modern French by former Situationist Alice Becker-Ho (Alice Debord), whose work on dangerous class slang & etymology gives her a unique expertise in handling these texts. My translations, – variations, really – are based on her book *La Part Maudite dans l'Oevure de François Villon* (Éditions L'échappée, 2018). I also refer readers to her other works in English *The Princes of Jargon, & The Essence of Jargon.*

I

Boarding a bus leaving Regret City
where the dupes work & marry
(save the Redhead who eludes the Watch)
around five or six of us were identified
by Premier Word & His Investigators.
We'd let the Zef dry up & get hard
core. Twenty Two for the Big Heavy
who'll come to circumcise your ears!
All good for the Big Leap Without a Future?
Twenty Two inches to the end of the Rope!

Get your kicks in, but Mind your Hoods!
Geolocate where the Eyes are perched
then spin straight to the Ferry & sail away
before you're added to the Wedding List
to be bound tighter than a Rope Bunny!
Rebigues moy tost ces enterveux
Show off those big Ears up close
with your middle finger pointed
where you're supposed to be wedded
Twenty Two inches to the end of the Rope!

Set aside your decoder picks
because a Kiss with a bite is rough
as doing Humble on the straw, taking it
in the hole, boxed up, laden with chains.
I say set sail, don't be Nuts!
The Heat will hang you out to dry!
Keep your feelings to yourself but
don't stop your distracting chatter.
You wear pants in order to wash them!
Twenty Two inches to the end of the Rope!

Comrades, cheats with dice & tools
some dudes & chicks be snitchy bitches!
Be careful not to get a sick Dick
because the worst can happen
Twenty Two inches from the end of the Rope!

II

Comrade Coco is on the lam
Samois is calling her to say
don't just give it up & come
for some cookie-cutter-turn-rat
to the kêrels & start singing
Poor Slut for Bruno-chilling-
by-the-pool-Latour, else
the hangman break your neck.

Change your look
watch your way when rolling
& head straight to the sticks
before you're the Writer in Res
at Matsqui where you'll be held
up high to sing like a bard until
the hangman breaks your neck.

Joyous comrades, experts in loading
the dice to keep the Nine at bay –
trick the Rabble without delay
watch the White Knights tweet &
try to gag you with their plumes
stupid cocks watching the Wires
so very far from earth until
the hangman breaks their necks.

Homeslices: drop your arms
toss the toonies you've plucked
lest you leave skin on the keys
& the hangman breaks your neck.

III

Cheaters at the Game
who at all times
fill their Cups with
the best booze
& at evening's turn
skin the dumb Fucks
to better place their wagers.
The Mugs, relieved of their silver
without tears & without pain stay
right where they've been planted;
these Gents who know so much.

Often in bed
they mean to leave their mark
but they're in our Trap!
Gas, grass or ass
Nobody rides for free!
Our accomplices are Deviants
who'll roll you like a pair of aces.
We're all making hay
two or three knocks to the head
& they'll be put back to bed
these Gents who know so much!

That's why, you boobs
Coquillards
keep an eye on the 22nd floor
where they'll give you a raise
your ass will not forget
& cross the line.
You'll be fucked over
 & come to understand
the costs incurred by Parrots
Surprised
& seized
by those miserable Pigs
those gents who know so much.

For fear of the Law's wood
& for fear of the prison's wool
reverse the rules of the Game
& its Mystifications
& don't get put in place
By these gents who know so much!

IV

Wired cheats playing at night
to pocket those beautiful Crowns
log your earnings elsewhere.
The Quarterbucks work with the cops!
Clever Karens run out of luck
Everyone Yapping is in cahoots
Three can keep a secret if two are dead
so beware of those basement Scrubs.

Bounce if you're identified
by Those Agents of the Take Down
without delay, ditch your coats
before you're in the Hangman's sights!
Separated from your breath
Stood up all stiff & tall
Protect your Neck against those
Fucking assholes!

The fools will be caught
& head straight to the gibbet.
Nothing matters once harpooned
The rope with four threads
Stretches & makes a face
Where the throat is dry
& the slippery tongue sticks out
At lowest of the low.

Colleagues, clever workers with words
Your Accomplices are not Professionals
Only *Suspects* of cheating the Game
So watch you don't end up in a ditch.

V

Cheaters cheating cheats
take a good look at your teachers
or you-know-who will mount
your derrière & put a ring on your
neck. Seriously you'll be sorry
if you don't "widen your stride"
& save your hide before
the Hangman ends your poem.

Bend against hocus-pocus fairies
Who bend time like Debussy Trap
Nestling with the IOC riff-raff
Angels, agents, & asses all.
Severin can't rap if he's dead
Like you, if you're the Watched
Three more Migos before you're home
& the Hangman ends your poem.

Learn how to translate the song
Don't hesitate to use the Three Modes or
Let the door hit your Ass on the way
Out. White skin won't help so die
on that Hill if you want. Nothing to
smell here except your own nose.
Better change your Handles quickly
Before the Hangman ends your poem.

Lords, fellow doers of crime
Do not marry one another
To you, I say stay vigilant
Until the Hangman ends your poem.

Rondel

Cool thing on the street
Let's go to the pool!

Come & play
Cool thing on the street

We'll get undressed
& soak in the hot tub

Cool thing on the street
Let's go to the pool!

Ballad in A Minor

It's queer to see Kundalini la-li-loongs!
queer when chummage is paid with prosage!
queer this pygia after a chirospasm!
queer when Chippy wears those taupe talarias!
queer to catch a phillyloo with arsefoot!
queer: a peruker with a codpiece!
queer: a wimpy in a free fire zone!
So queer to cry "Papa" when he comes!

It's queer to ffagott when you're uxorilocal!
queer the arch dell dodging the espantoon!
queer to spy a kaha riding in a copper punt!
queer: when that muttnik cries *prang!* PRANG!
queer: using "banana stick" as a varnarbi!
queer to hear wazzums from Big Joe in Boston!
queer from Little Joe in Renton too!
So queer to cry "Papa" when he comes!

It's queer to smell axle grease on a line-load!
queer when a peter funk meets a cinder bull!
queer: a botany bay dozen from a peek freak!
queer: those genuffling W.U.M.P.S!
queer to read Žižek in a wappenschawing!
queer: the funkum on the poultice plumber!
queer when Schneider wears a fumadiddie!
So queer to cry "Papa" when he comes!

It's queer: a scag jones poose!
queer to find a pretzel bender playing crack-a-loo!
queer when mamoose rain-maker has a sky-hoot!
queer when a punk-boy finds a flopper stopper!
queer to kyoodle in a laconium! A *laconium*!
queer the second dicky is so ooly-drooly!
queer hoochie-papping stot you got there!
So queer to cry "Papa" when he comes!

Friends, it's all so queer!
It's queer to grease a molly!
& queer that Ticklepecker!
So queer to cry "Papa" when you come!

Leprosy was considered an STI in 1463. Boys were thought to be safer than women. Women were not permitted to sodomize each other.

Regarding the erotic life of the dangerous classes, Alice Becker Ho observes "there is no such thing as sexual taboo in a world where everything there is to know on the subject is common knowledge."

24

I don't feel I've overspent
on booze & drugs & hotels

& nothing's been pawned
for Love, nothing my friends will notice

anyway, nothing that cost them a dime.
I'll speak my mind & my word is my bond:

The rumours against me are false –
one who is not guilty does not confess.

The Coquillards were accused of crimes such as B&E, impersonation, counterfeiting, fencing stolen goods, theft, fraudulent trading of meat, horse stealing, cheating at cards, murder, and pickpocketing. Testimony against them was collected from smiths, prostitutes, barbers, and taverners. Prosecutors tried to flip members in custody, but they said they'd rather suffer as prisoners than die at the hands of their Friends.

They took oaths, and shared their profits. They had custom tools for picking locks fabricated.

Ballad of Negations

Never hoop a horn mad fancy man
Never muzzle a bawdy basket with a cheeser
Never pop a shanker on a bob-tail
Never snivel if your article snilches a charm
Never cap verses with a distracted division
Never nose a rum bite ama-glug-glug
Unless you're keen to polish the King's irons
Never tell them your name!

Never stick your plug tail in a mouse trap
Never trade trinkets with a word pecker
Never share your lobscouse with a crook shank
Never bilk in a flash panney
Never yowl at a chalker's fartleberries
Never set fambles on a town bull
Unless you're a little pork crying woolbird
Never tell them your name!

Never nip a dandy prat with your ruffles
Never crib from Captain Copperthorne's Crew
Never occupy a goosecap
Never mung to a Jack in the Office
Never plant the books with a boung nipper
Never todge a Dimber Damber
Unless you want a ride on a wooden horse
Never, ever, tell them your name!

Despite his intimate knowledge of the events, Villon's name does not appear in the extensive police records kept on the violent student/police riots that shook Paris in May, 1453. Unfortunately, his poetic account – "copied in a notebook and stashed under the table" – of this significant historical moment has either disappeared, or been coded into some other text now hiding in plain view.

Villon,

I believe I have some obligation to honour the life of the man who wrote your poems. But this life is a *diablerie* that appears only in the arrangement of the *bric-a-brac* found in the poems themselves. &, I suppose, your court records.

There's a question here around testimony & veracity. You are sometimes referred to by your contemporaries as "so-called Villon". Your accomplices did not have names either – "Little John *known* as the Spaniard" or "Oudet Durax *known as* 'of Bordeaux'". If there is a life to be translated here, I believe it can only be found in the perspective of the alias.

This is what "is known":

— You were born on April Fools Day, 1431, & assigned a name which is no longer your name. Your literary notoriety is founded on a poem posing as a legal document (a will), in which you leave things you don't have to people you don't know. The poem also functions as a map of 15th century Paris where taverns are wayfinders. You swear on the authenticity of this *Testament* on one testicle, but you don't indicate which, *dexter* or *sinister*.

— You were charged with murdering a priest, & convicted of several robberies. Your first editors felt that the language in certain of your *Ballads* was unintelligible & suggested an uncomfortable proximity to organized crime.

— You were sentenced to death on several occasions before finally being banished from Paris in 1463. The biography ends like that: not with death, which is what your poems promise, but with a *disappearance*. I imagine you were mauled by bear, or boar. Perhaps you are still alive.

— In the 15th century, one could be tortured for various types of fraud, such as inducing a miscarriage or being homosexual. In 1457, a Coquillard was boiled in oil in public for counterfeiting.

Low throwing dice were fashioned from bone, wood, & pewter. Swapping them in & out of one's hand during a game of *risque* is a delicate skill.

"Villon," I've been working on these poems for some time now – since Vespers at least – & I'm certain I have made no progress at all.

>Please take pity on poor Roger.
>— RF

18

Why charge me with theft?
Just because I hide a little piracy

By foaming at the mouth? If only
I could arm myself like you

I'd also be The Prince of Pigs.

It's worth pausing on the fact that those who enforce the Law also use disguises and ruses to conceal their identities.

Danse Macabre
From *Le Testament*

161

This isn't the place for games.
What good to be staggeringly rich

to fool around in King size beds
chug booze & engorge the belly

hit all the parties, festivals & clubs
call every hour happy-hour? For

if all pleasure desires eternity
life is a hangover without end

162

& when I consider the heads
of bodies stacked in the *charniers*

notice they are also Heads of
State & Support Staff, Judges &

Cops, Small Business Owners
Etc., I can swap one for the other

Politicians for Activists
I don't see any difference

163

between those heads that declined
to other heads or those that when

still alive held themselves high
feared by some, served by others

I see them all in their final scene
assembled in a heap, pell mell

all singularities stripped away —
neither Slave nor Master here.

As a result of the Black Death, by the 1400's the Holy Innocents' Cemetery was so crowded that the citizens of Paris, to make room for the city's future dead, constructed *charniers* (from the Latin *carnarium*, or "place for meat") to lodge surplus remains. The walls of this charnel house where bones were sorted and stacked were adorned with poems and scenes depicting the Dance of the Dead. The building was demolished in 1669, but a woodcut image of the mural depicts a dancing skeleton *still wearing his crown*. While observing this figure one cold morning in October, Villon composed these lines.

Ballad of the Fourth Mode

Hello Jabbering Birds! Messy things go
"Who's gonna pay for a coulis spoon in NYC
It's a pleasure to sing-along in a *Ballad*
Such great feet print prank to sink a pink seven
That's some buffoon poopy poop there homie
Cool slob on a foot long gong goozler homie
Dribble fast if Ol' Stack wants to talk or suck
On vintage car day & teh old Cali collar
So brew some gagaku tuneage in the end"
Going shacky whacky in Florida you see

Show is on they say "it's the Super Bowl
Shed Eight Tears for the Waffle Temple
Just a sheet of toast for this Sore-bone s.v.p
Queen Níðhöggr I miss your spangles &
Your glucose sack nest with White custard
She grew up fast in that baby carrier
Ripping up quinoa toast while sitting in
For the monsters Daequan loves are three
Times the coke on Saudi Airlines Flight 282"
Going shacky whacky on Galiano for free

Plotting for that Super Bowl show homie
Southpaw Debbie's sensi brings me down
Like the APC & soon she's all "delusional
National aqua chattis are gross mooses
Cherry swab pointing to tears drunk in

Funcanny Valley what a face the MLA has
Now the song gears new swabs in Doré's
Hey Baby he's got Toys 4 Euros oh yes
Desires pour in when Jesus shoots his phun"
Gone sugar shacky in Oakland you see

Smiley Cyprus singing at halftime homie
Highlights can be ordered via the Party
Level up if you want to swallow three
If graffiti could vote it would vote for me
& here's a final shack line just for thee

In 1444 the brittle remnants of Christ's foreskin were brought to Paris. A great many miracles occurred.

39

I'm certain that poor & rich
& profs & proles & cops & robbers

& yuppies & lumpen & lushes &
& prudes & big & little & straight

& queer babes in parkas with
top buns & yoga mats & data plans

whatever their bank statements say
marriage will seize them all.

When women killed their husbands in 15th century France, they were accused of *treason*, not murder.

63

& I suppose – without meaning
any disrespect to women –

that it's *nature femininne*
to want to spread one's

love to others & though I pause
when putting this in a poem

I have also heard it said
in town & further West

on certain islands, that love
comes best in multiples of three.

This remarkable, if brief, *huitain* may be the most eloquent case against the couple-form left to us from the Medieval period.

Candles were expensive in the 15th century, so it was not uncommon to find oneself accidentally in bed with someone other than one's spouse, nor to retire to bed in the dark only to discover one's spouse already in the arms of a friend or neighbour who had lost their way.

BL MSS Royal 1 D X f. 2v

Villon,

Imagine getting up from your desk, going to a bar & finding there one or two other poets interested in discussing each other's poetry. They criticize the vapid work of their contemporaries, pass along the details of the various scandals, affairs, betrayals, & failures that define their milieu, discuss the costs of living in their city.

Perhaps you had some familiarity with this, as I did, before you fled. But this morning, as my son sleeps in my bed, which he came to in the middle of the night after a dream startled him, I am looking out at the dark trees & listening to the last few birds jabbering after their chorus at dawn, & I can't imagine myself in such a bar. I am far away from that now & have been for many years. Here, I don't talk to poets in the bars. I'm sure you understand.

In my last letter I said something about the perspective of the *alias*. I made this observation before I read about the aftermath of the incident with the priest, where you used the name "Mouton" in your report. Then I saw this "Mouton" turn up in your poem, as though he were an actual person. I see you use this trick of swapping names again & again, as if this were the shell game of some *mountebank*.

Villon, I'm rereading our *Passages from "Le Lais"*. I know you were not in your room at Vespers, listening to the bells of the Sorbonne, composing intellectual poems citing the academic ideas of the day: you were in a tavern, with your crew, conspiring to rob the College of Navarre across town. The poem is an *alibi* that leads at once to, & away from, the truth.

Alias & alibi: I believe these may be the rossignols I need to crack your poems.

  — RF

Passages from "Le Lais"

In the last instance, writing
this evening, solitary (it's all good)

& using the practice of dictation
I heard the bells toll from the

University (they always seem
to chime when something new

arrives) so I stopped what I was
doing to do what I'd been taught

& thus my troubles began (this
had nothing to do with the booze) –

my intellect was *arrêté*. My RAM
had failed. I had no storage left

for Semantic nor Episodic info
nor any other big ideas, like

the Theory of Interpellation
derived from the Orders

of the Symbolic, the Imaginary
& the Real & from which

the Subject ("me") is barred
(I'm sure I read this in Althusser).

But then the Aesthetic stirred
& endowed my Imagination

such that the Sovereign "I"
once detained, then slain, by

a disremembered Repression
that had apprehended every part

of me, awoke, to demonstrate
how one's Self is seized.

& then at last when my mixed up
mind untwined & found repose

the screen froze & the lights shut off
& there was not another thing

to say. So I hit the sack, muffled.

December, 1456. The poem locates the poet in his room on the Porte Rouge at the moment the bells rang at the Sorbonne, a somber sound which prompts him to recall certain concepts he had learned while a student at the University of Paris.

However, two years later, an associate of the poet's would confess that on this day, and at this time, Villon was in fact in a tavern with three known Coquillards, plotting the robbery of the Faculty of Theology at the College of Navarre.

Needless to say, the authorities accepted as Truth the *confession*, not the poem.

90

Also, for my Love, an *actual* rose
not my broken heart or liver

for she's already chosen another
organ & she's got plenty of assets

plus a grant. Yes, her soft leather
purse is deep & wide & open but

don't try to own her head or her ass
she's not the marrying type (I tried).

16

Friends, if our deaths were
in the public interest, or even

the milieu's, surely we would
"tie the knot." But having judged

ourselves we know we don't
sweat the young, nor the old

the emerging, nor the nearly dead.
A man with dialectics can't move

language forwards or backwards
– it simply won't budge.

Villon,

For me, you are like an ancient city bombed out by the Enlightenment. & I'm not sure I need an ancient city bombed out by the Enlightenment in my life right now.

Our season together took a turn when I caught you cheating.

It's not that I don't love you. It's just that this game is interminable, & history is catching up with us. You can hear it between every line, *Omnes ergo in unum positi compleant.*

It's true, we've had some epic times drinking together. You have eyes like old cabbages, & the most hoary ass I've ever seen. Your language is like a savoury duck with pears, poached & gleaned, brawling with my tongue. When I see you gambling with CC et al., it makes me want to steal the purse & lodge us for a week at the Sylvia.

Instead I lie in bed alone at night wishing you were a Prince, & not a Thief who likes to fuck with my poems.

What I'm trying to say, is *prends tes poems de cul de pute et vas-y.*

    Yours no more,
    — RF

Rondel

Later – I'm going to cry
See ya – baby
Sayonara – to elevated beauty
Bye-bye – the lamest of good-byes
Au revoir – with many x's & o's
I'll just leave you to lay there.

Adieu – I'm actually crying now
Adios – for the misery you caused
Is more than I can say here
But if I'm being sincere
Yes, I've wasted my words so
So long – this is my final good-bye!

On 3 January, 1463, Parliment is persuaded by Villon's Appeal to commute his death-sentence to banishment from Paris for ten years. He vanishes from history.

159

I'm speaking to you, my
comrades in pleasure –

be on guard against visibility
for it kills by excessive light.

Evade it. It's bad for your body.
Keep moving. Avoid milieus

& for Christ's sake never
forget we're all going to die.

In an age where life is represented as nothing but a brief and miserable respite from death, the most radical act possible would be not to die, but *to disappear*.

Or: "Rebigues moy cost ces enterveux."

Acknowledgements

I was introduced to Villon by Alice Becker-Ho while working on the critical introduction to her *Essence of Jargon*, with expert translator John McHale in 2009. I began working on *After Villon* shortly after, publishing occasional poems here & there. So this book reflects over a decade of engagement with Villon's life & work. Along the way, I have been in contact with many fellow travellers, & have benefitted from innumerable translations, articles, & studies.

The literature surrounding Villon's work is vast, but I would direct interested English speaking readers to translations by Sargent-Baur, Georgi, Callais/Rodefer, & Kinnel. Aubrey Burl's *Dance Macabre: Francois Villon, Poetry, & Murder in Medieval France*, a lively & sensational account of Villon's life, makes for a good soundtrack.

Readers with a deeper interest in Villon might enjoy Alice Becker-Ho's *La Part Maudite Dans L'Ouvre de Francois Villion*, Thierry Martin's *Villon: Ballades en Argot Homosexual*, *Le Jargon de Villon ou Le Gai Savoir de la Coquille*, by Pierre Guiraud, & Tristan Tzara's *The Secret of Villon*.

My translations & variations are indebted to all these texts, & others, but they remain my own. I take full responsibility for their extraordinary errors.

I wish to acknowledge the support of BC Arts Council & the Canada Council for the Arts in the research & creation of this book.

Selections from *After Villon* have appeared in *The Capilano Review, Distinctively Dionysian, The Oystercatcher, SOME Magazine,* & *Tripwire*. Thanks to the editors of those publications. Thanks also to Melissa, Oliver, and Rolf at the indefatigable New Star Books; and to Dianna Bonder for the illustration on p. 31, among other vital contributions.

Lastly I thank my friends, lovers, & partner in crime. I won't give you up here. You know who you are.